There is a sacredness in tears. They are not the mark of weakness, but of power. They speak more eloquently than ten thousand tongues. They are the messengers of overwhelming grief, of deep contrition, and unspeakable love.

Washington Irving

Healthy Grieving:
An Opportunity for Growth

A Collection of Essays

First Edition

Healthy Grieving:
An Opportunity for Growth

A Collection of Essays

Dedication

We dedicate this book to family, friends, and professionals who devote themselves to help those who grieve. Thank you for your kindness, generosity, resilience, and insight.

Acknowledgements

To Jack Holland, friend and student of Lem, who prepared this work for publication.

To Estin Kiger, Tai Chi teacher and artist, who designed the front and back cover.

To Charlene Ide Flanter for guidance with the Hawaii Lantern Floating Festival.

To Pat Kirtley, our editor, for harmonizing the work of five authors.

To Rev. Felix Vistal for his insights into Filipino culture.

To the Fabulous Five for dedication, cooperation, and determination.

Thank You!

Healthy Grieving:
An Opportunity for Growth

A Collection of Essays

by

Patricia M. Kirtley
Lem Londos Railsback
William M. Kirtley
William R. Curtis
Terry L. Lovelace

Contents

Introduction

Each author presents an essay that views this amorphous and difficult topic from a different standpoint. The first paper presents a heartfelt discussion of how people cope with grief. The second essay is a clear and comprehensive examination of the stages of grief. The third section conveys the beauty and emotion of the Lantern Floating Ceremony in Hawaii, a syncretic event that features Native Hawaiian, Buddhist, and Japanese bereavement rituals. The last two essays describe a variety of interesting funeral rites representative of different cultures.

Good Grief!

What is "Good Grief"? The immediate response of many will undoubtedly include visions of Charles Schulz's "funny round-headed kid" staring straight up while flat on his back after falling for Lucy's football ruse...AGAIN!

Like Charlie Brown, human beings have many experiences with grief. These do not always involve an actual death. Countless losses produce grief. A lost job, the destruction after a fire or a deadly storm, even moving to a new city can trigger anguish and sorrow. But what is good grief especially in regard to the loss of a loved one? Or perhaps, how should we process it? The answer certainly isn't, "Get over it!" or "Just deal!" One answer is simple. Life is unpredictable and the cultivation of an open heart and open mind to the present, positive elements in our lives empowers us to deal with our grief and the grief of others.

Buddhist psychologist Sameet M. Kumar, in *grieving mindfully* (2005) discusses several general types of grief. No matter how large or small, these occurrences can threaten our sense of security. Most people seek stability in their lives. Change is difficult, even if it may be rewarding. A simple detour or a neighbor's unavailability for emergency childcare may cause frustration and anxiety. On a deeper level, the death of a loved one brings sadness and often disturbs an individual's well being. It jars constancy not only physically, but also mentally and emotionally. "Grief is a part of life, and, like life, it is unpredictable" (Kumar p. 43).

There are basically two types of loss of life. The first is sudden and totally unexpected. This may be an accident, the result of a violent crime, or suicide. Such an event brings more questions than answers. All communication with that individual is gone and that loss leaves those who remain with uncertainty. Could an intervention have prevented the outcome? Could a phone call have helped? What if? What if? There are no answers for those who remain.

The second type of loss is gradual as a result of aging or a lingering physical or mental illness. This gives those who remain, time to communicate and clarify. This may seem to many to be preferable to a sudden loss, but both types are difficult and disconcerting. It is agonizing for friends and especially caregivers to experience this pending loss as it slowly progresses to its inevitable conclusion. They might even long for a cessation of the daily pain. This is normal and fairly common, although the aftermath often is a nearly overwhelming guilt that may require personal expiation.

A gradual loss may also bring familial conflict in making end of life decisions. These choices require thoughtful communication and sensitivity as well as a focus on the emotional needs of all family members in making cooperative and inclusive decisions. This concern should incorporate the needs of the loved one as well as the wishes of those who will ultimately function as a supportive unit.

Regardless of the type of loss, one primary human need is closure, a requirement for stability. Unless there is a recorded or written communication, it is impossible to know what was in the minds of the victims of sudden death and no direct means of communication exists. However, in gradual or ongoing loss, there is a possibility of closure through caring communication. Family members and friends have an opportunity to heal and harvest: healing any misconceptions and imagined or real affronts and harvesting the joy of shared memories.

In palliative care physician Dr. Ira Byock's book, *Dying Well: Peace and Possibilities at the End of Life* (1997), an essay by Stephen Morris lists five statements hospice recommends for patients to facilitate closure and strengthen personal relationships: (1) "I am sorry." (2) "I forgive you." (3) "I love you." (4) "Thank you." and (5) "Good-bye." (p. 140). Discussing these five affirmations with a loved one is the ideal situation; yet, even in the case of an unexpected death, taking time to mindfully ponder these five declarations can provide comfort, relief, and closure for the aggrieved.

Psychologist Robert Niemeyer (1997) states, "Even if we may feel as if grief is something that has been forced upon us, or to which we are being subjected, it is actually something in which we actively participate" (as cited in Kumar p. 83). The world changes for those who grieve.

Recognition of this allows acceptance of a new reality.

Those who grieve experience both mental and even physical pain. Some may seek to avoid that discomfort by using alcohol, medication, or succumb to another addiction. Unfortunately, these prove to be little more than distractions. The answers are within. The pain of grief is not a weakness. It is the result of caring, of opening up to another, of being vulnerable, of being willing to love.

Many find solace in the spirituality of religious teachings. Renowned Oxford scholar and Christian author of *The Chronicles of Narnia, the Screwtape Letters,* and *Mere Christianity*, C. S. Lewis, wrote an impassioned diary of his grief after the loss of his wife, Joy Davidman. Hers was a lingering death from cancer and he was her only caregiver at the end. In *A Grief Observed* (1961), Lewis initially rails at the Almighty, angry that when he experienced joy, God seemed to welcome him with open arms. Yet, when he was completely desperate, there was no answer. It appeared that God totally ignored him, slammed the door in his face, and threw the bolt (p. 6).

Lewis passes through every stage of grief and eloquently expresses his frustration, depression, and anger. In a foreword to Lewis's book, noted children's author Madeline L'Engle writes that she is grateful to Lewis for his courage "to yell, to doubt, to kick at God with angry violence" (p. xvi). The aggravation expressed by this great Christian apologist "gives us permission to admit our own doubts, our own angers and anguishes, and to know that they are part of the soul's growth" (p. xvi).

Lewis realized that "bereavement is an integral part of love" (p.50). He even asks God if, in order to meet his wife again, he should learn to love Him so much that he will not care if he meets her in the afterlife (p. 68). He concluded that his journey led him to believe that God did not slam the door in his face, but rather shook His head in loving frustration that Lewis simply could not understand the entire concept of death (p. 69).

In June 1983, a long-distance phone call changed Christian philosopher, Dr. Nicholas Wolterstorff's life. His twenty-five year old son died in a mountain-climbing accident in Austria. This totally unexpected end to his robust son's life was a shattering experience. He recorded his thoughts in a diary, published as *Lament for a Son* (1987). Most expressions of sorrow are heart-rending but the author wrote this small volume "in the hope that some of those who sit beside us on the mourning bench for children would find my words giving voice to their own honoring and grieving" (p. 5).

As a professor of Philosophical Theology at Yale University, Dr. Wolterstorff was fully aware of the spiritual aspects of the impermanence of life. His son's death engendered a deep and lasting pain, causing him to examine his own relationship to his God. "There's a hole in the world now. In the place where he was, there's now just nothing" (p. 33). He embraced Gerard Manley Hopkins' inscape, the essence of life. "And one child's death differs from another not in the intensity of the pain it causes but in the quality" (p. 24).

Wolterstorff shares what comforted him in his grief. He cautions those who would say that they knew how he felt. They didn't. He asked that people not tell him that it was not so bad. It was. Some said that they really had nothing to say but wanted to express their caring for him in his sorrow. He, and all who mourn, needed that. What he, and most who bear the pain of a death required was an honest expression of caring. "What words can do is testify that there is more than pain in our journey on earth to a new day. Of those things that are more, the greatest is love" (p. 34).

Wolterstorff mentions C. S. Lewis being angry with God and comments that he is not as angry as he is hurt. "My wounds are an unanswered question. The wounds of all humanity are an unanswered question" (p. 68). In the end, Wolterstorff makes peace with God and concludes that his suffering has refined him. "In the valley of suffering, despair and bitterness are brewed. But there also character is made. The valley of suffering is the vale of soul-making" (p. 97).

The message of these texts seems new, regardless of the dates of the deaths they chronicle. Perhaps with grief, like violent injuries, the scarring is always fragile and the angry wound remains just below the surface. Spirituality is obviously helpful but, in itself, is no protection against the ravages of grief. For many, as Wolterstorff stated,

"Faith is a footbridge that you don't know will hold you up over the chasm until you are forced to walk out onto it" (p. 76).

What is the answer? Is "Good Grief" truly the ultimate oxymoron? Most literature on grief suggests one solution, one means of coping that appears to lessen the pain and strengthen the mourner. That solution is simple but challenging. Kumar states, "grief ultimately teaches everyone the same lesson: to value the relationships, experiences, and time that you have in the present moment" (p. 22). Wolterstorff says, "We do not treasure each other enough" (p. 13). C. S. Lewis concludes, "bereavement is a universal and integral part of our experience of love" (p. 59).

Both Lewis and Wolterstorff used writing as an outlet for their grief. Any active participation to honor deceased friends and family can be cathartic. Friends of cancer patients may participate in community walks or races dedicated to their loved ones. Both physical activities and creative endeavors offer solace and consolation.

Each mourner's experience is unique because each mourner is unique.

Mindfulness, meditation, or even carving out a few moments of quiet time will provide the opportunity for acceptance. One powerful solution to the pain is to value each moment, each hour, each day; each year we share with loved ones. Acknowledge their faults and failings as well as their treasure. In this there is comfort. There will still be pain at their passing, but let the richness of memories be balm to the suffering. Over time, that will be a gift, both to those who are physically gone as well as those who remain. Indeed, that will be good grief.

The Stages of Grief

Except for infants who die in the womb, infants who die at childbirth, and infants who die shortly thereafter, all humans apparently suffer grief. In other words, to be human is to suffer grief, probably many times within a single lifetime. The very ancient prehistoric humans suffered grief; the hunting and gathering and wandering humans suffered grief; the early humans living in stable groups in particular sites suffered grief; and the latter fully developed Homo sapiens suffered grief. Grief is a part of human living. Because it was recognized as such so many eons ago, the Greeks institutionalized the notion in their goat/"tragos"/tragedy mask for their outdoor dramas.

A wag noted that man is the only creature that laughs while everything else above and below remains serious: hence, the comedy mask of the Greeks. The other mask/side of the coin is that humans suffer grief at one time or another or at several times within each single life. The interplay between comedy for the happy times and grief for the unhappy times provided directional focus for the Greek audiences. In today's world, both happy and unhappy times chart each human life.

Grief occurs in every culture around the world. It occurs to humans regardless of their social status, economic level, racial background, height, weight, nationality, gender, sexual preference, ability/disability, educational attainment or lack thereof, membership in any political party, or color of hair. Grief comes to all. It arrives whenever one discovers that one is about to die from complications from old age and/or an incurable illness. Grief comes when a loved one dies, as when a father dies, for example. Grief comes when a highly valued individual dies—a beloved president like JFK. Grief comes when a much-loved pet dies—a pet mutt who has lived for fifteen years in one's household. Grief can come also at a breakup of lovers, at the disappointment of losing one's long-held job, at hearing of an epidemic that killed so many babies. At one time or another, whenever a sadly dramatic change in our lives occurs, grief descends upon each one of us.

Because the descent of grief is so universal, a close examination of the ailment and its processes may prove helpful to the reader. This examination begins with the famous "first of its kind" model put forth by the Swiss-American psychiatrist Elisabeth Kubler-Ross in 1969 with her book *On Death and Dying*. This essay examines several other collections of observations, analyses, and conclusions.

Kubler-Ross's extensive interviews and personal work with terminally ill patients over decades provided her with insights that she formally organized into five stages of grieving. She stressed that (1) not every grieving individual goes through all of the five stages, (2) that some grieving individuals may undergo only two or three stages; (3) that even though a grieving individual may "complete" a stage to go on to another, the individual may "return" to the earlier stage; (4) differing reactions by grieving individuals are determined by the personality and coping structures of each individual.

Denial and Isolation - Refusing to believe that one's own death is imminent, that a loved one has died, or that a strong positive in one's life will never be again is "hard to take," as they say, for just about everybody. Refusing to accept the onslaught of a new reality offers momentary comfort. After all, if one cannot face "full front" the total reality, then facing a small bit at a time allows the grieving person some time in which to accept gradually only what the grieving person can actually handle at a given moment. This denying may take a long time. One must handle it, piece by piece, in isolation. Intended solace from others often constitutes wasted time and may, in fact, interfere with the positive conclusion of this state.

Anger - Once the personal denying in solitude begins to fade, denial may turn into anger. The grieving individual may direct their anger toward the doctor who delivered the final diagnosis, namely, that the death of the grieving individual is eminent. They may direct their anger at the loved one who died, at other family members, at friends, and at objects. And even though the grieving individual realizes that it was not the doctor's fault for scientifically guessing what his tests have shown, that it was not the fault of the loved one who died to have left so early and so suddenly, that it was not the fault of any of those who are attempting to comfort, and/or that it was not the fault of the vanity mirror or the new micro-oven or the window pane, the grieving individual still seethes with anger. The grieving individual's contradiction between her/his logical understanding that the fault is misdirected and his/her emotional anger at the over-whelming situation eats away. One stays angry, one is angry over being angry, and one grows even more angry with one's anger. To move through this stage may require much time. The time taken to quiet the anger varies with each individual.

Bargaining - To overcome one's sense of vulnerability and emotional pain and to regain a sense of one's control over life, the grieving individual may entertain a series of "ifs": if I had gone to the clinic earlier; if I had talked more to my mother before she died; if I had just paid more attention to the signs; if I had been a better person; and so on. In attempting to bargain for a more palatable understanding, the grieving individual is attempting to heal.

Depression - The grieving individual may "come to grips" with the current situation—cost of a funeral, selection of flowers, how to distribute keepsakes, how to thank all those who have attempted to help. Also, the grieving individual may "come to grips" with the reality that one's death is eminent, that the loved one really is gone forever, that the celebrity or pet or lover or job is truly gone.

Acceptance - Finally, the grieving individual may reach a period of dignified calm withdrawal. As one accepts one's eminent demise, the lost of a loved one, a beloved celebrity, a lover, or job, the grieving individual finally "comes to rest" with the realization that the loss is real.

Kubler-Ross offered her insights to help medical professionals, psychiatric professionals, and workers with the terminally ill. As a result, the general public deals with the terminally ill in a more understanding, empathetic, and helpful way. Her work, especially her book, "...revolutionized how the American medical field takes care of the terminally ill" (Elisabeth Kubler-Ross Foundation, 2014). Dr, Allan Kellehear claimed that her book "...is one of the most important humanitarian works on the care of the dying written in the Western world" (Elisabeth Kubler-Ross Foundation, 2014).

Critics pointed to Kubler-Ross's "lack" of "regular" modern research protocols in her work. Readers should remember that Kubler-Ross never presented her book as a modern scientific research study with all possible safeguards; instead, she simply offered her many years of observations, descriptions, and reflections drawn from actual interviews with actual individuals over decades. Indeed, she was just trying to help.

Wishes on the Waves
Lantern Floating Hawaii

"We've all lost loved ones. We share common feelings," noted one person at last year's Lantern Floating Ceremony Hawaii ceremony (Tsai 2013). This annual event helps people access and process grief in an equally healthy way. Thousands gathered on Memorial Day at Ala Moana beach in Honolulu to honor their departed loved ones. Shinnyo-en Buddhism, through its secular arm the Na Lei Aloha Foundation, sponsored the ceremony. Lanterns were free and the ceremony was open to all, a gift to the community. The motto of the ceremony was Many Rivers, One Ocean – Friendship.

A review of the literature on ritual provided insights into the Lantern Floating Ceremony. Emile Durkheim (1965), an early Sociologist, argued that rituals were "schools of collective behavior" that unite the community and affirm the collective moral conscience (p. 170). Victor Turner, an English anthropologist, stated in *Drama,*

Fields, and Metaphors (1975), that rituals, "achieve genuinely cathartic effects" (p. 56). In his later work, *Ritual and Theater* (1982), Turner thought of ritual as performance (p. 79). Bernard Giesen, (2006), a Sociologist at the University of Konstanz agreed. He described ceremonies as "embodied performances, as events produced and, experienced bodily by actors in a shared situation and in a local site" (p. 342).

This paper uses the term "ceremony" to identify a formal act prescribed by ritual, protocol, or convention. "Rituals" are a part of a larger celebration. They provoke a sense of awe of the sacred and follow established customs and traditions (Henslin p. GL-10). This paper uses the word "signal" in the limited sense of a sound or action that announces the beginning of a ceremony.

Hawaiian and Japanese cultures provide a plethora of ceremonies replete with signals and symbols. The blowing of the conch shell (Pu) announced the beginning of the Lantern Floating Hawaii Ceremony. Thousands of candle-lit lanterns, each a vessel of its own, symbolize "a soul set free, a grief let go, or a loved one that will never fade" (Zoelick, 2012, p. A6 c. 2).

This essay examines how this process of healthy grieving heals people through a personal and collective moment of remembrance.

Originally Memorial Day honored the men and women who died serving in the Armed Forces of the United States. In the last decade, people have expanded the scope of this holiday to include all who have passed. Shinnyo-en volunteers dispersed 6000 lantern kits on 26 May 2014, at 10:00 AM. The line for the bags containing individual lanterns was long, but the line for the collective remembrance was short. Participants wrote the names of their loved ones for inclusion on both types of lanterns that they would launch at sundown. The process of dealing with grief had begun.

Many participants spent the entire day at the park with family and friends sharing stories and meals, celebrating and remembering together. Justin Goshi, a Shinnyo-en volunteer, observed that the ceremony attracted participants because it crossed boundaries, religions, beliefs, and backgrounds (Davis 2014). Some people traveled long distances to take part. More than fifty thousand people gathered on the beach, according to news accounts. Roy Ho, Executive Director of Na Lei Aloha Foundation, observed that even though there were a large number of people present, "there's somehow a moment to yourself" (Davis 2014).

The Floating Lantern Ceremony Hawaii followed certain literary conventions. Aristotle in his *Poetics* described dramatic story as "a whole with a beginning, middle, and end" (p. 1450b27). In the evening, two events signaled the official start of the Lantern Floating Hawaii. Hau'oli Akaka sang a traditional oli or chant, filled with the power of words and alive with complex allusions. The Shinnyo Taiko Ensemble unleashed the pulsating throb of Taiko drumming.

A series of Interviews, testimonials, and a short video interview with Shinso Ito, the leader of Shinnyo-en, gave people the background and history of the ceremony. Her Holiness reminded her listeners that, the act of floating lanterns was an individual and collective action that symbolized "our intention to put our thoughts into action" (Vimeo Video, 2014). She urged, "Do not let such moments be short lived, find a way to make it lasting" (Vimeo Video, 2014).

Del Beazley, lead singer for the Makaha Sons, a popular Hawaiian group, performed a heartfelt version of "I'll remember you," a tribute to one of the band members who recently died. The Shinnyo Taiko Ensemble, accompanied by an electronic violin and other instruments, followed with another poignant number. At this dramatic moment, volunteers carried six large parent lanterns containing prayers for all humans to the center of the stage.

A Buddhist priest set a large lighted brass lantern on the altar, a sign of truth and a signal that Her Holiness Shinso Ito was about to deliver her remarks. Resplendent in an embroidered red silk robe and carrying a folded fan, she stepped to the podium. She reminded the audience, "Our acts of lighting lanterns today is one of remembrance and of giving concrete expression to our gratitude. It is also an opportunity, a source of inspiration, for awakening ourselves to our inner light" (Vimeo Video, 2014).

The program paid homage to community leaders, who lit the light of harmony with torches. Video clips played their pre-recoded comments on the large screen above the stage. Kirk Caldwell, Mayor of the City and County of Honolulu, stated that the celebration fostered a connectedness that transcends all differences (Vimeo Video, 2014). The program also recognized the hula, the iconic dance of Hawaii. Hau'oli Akaka chanted an introduction to the Halau Hula Kamamolikolehu, a dance group. In response, these young women clad in white blouses and bright blue floor length skirts danced a graceful hula.

Her Holiness Shinso Ito rang a small bell at 7:00 p.m. alerting the audience that the climax for the ceremony was about to begin. Families moved to the front of the crowd, put their lanterns in the sea, and let go of their sorrow. A member of the Taiko Ensemble struck a large bowl-shaped gong. Its deep reverberating sound echoed down the beach. The Shinnyo-en Shonyo ensemble under the direction of Martin Hosch played a haunting melody that fused the powerful rhythm of a traditional Buddhist chant with a Western choral arrangement.

Her Holiness Shinso Ito blessed the lanterns and those in attendance. A subordinate priest mixed rice and water, a ritual called Onjiki, a symbol of sending nourishment to the departed. Eight young women strew flower petals over the stage and along the path to the sea, the Sanje ritual. Torchbearers led the way for volunteers who carried the six parent lanterns to a landing, where assistants took them aboard boats for placement in the sea. Her Holiness Shinso Ito looked on, calm and serene.

The ceremony closed with an instrumental number and final song by the participants. Her Holiness joined hands with two children and sang *Hawai'i Aloha*, considered an anthem by the Hawaiian people. The chorus of the song, "Oli e! Oli e!" urged the youth of Hawaii to rejoice. Later in the evening, out of respect for the environment, Shinnyo-en volunteers retrieved all the lanterns. They will clean and repair them for next year's ceremony.

The Lantern Floating Ceremony presented the audience with individual and collective stories which, taken together, had a synergistic effect. Signaling events like the blowing of the conch shell, Taiko drumming, Native Hawaiian chants, and the ringing of the bell, alerted the audience that something sacred was about to happen. The narrators moved the program seamlessly from one ritual to the next until the climax of the story, the floating of parent and individual lanterns. Her Holiness clearly described Shinnyo-en Buddhism's belief in enlightenment through public service. Her healing words framed the ceremony with the promise of the victory of life over death.

Some cultures allow people to grieve freely and openly; others are more reserved. The Lantern Floating Ceremony provided an environment in which those in attendance felt free to express emotion. Each element of the ceremony united everyone through sight and sound. A combination of effects dissolved people's patina of reserve and allowed them to grieve in a healthy way. The ceremony allowed many to express their grief, an act that will continue into the future, and a gift warmly received and graciously acknowledged.

Native American Funeral and Mourning Practices

The Bureau of Indian Affairs (BIA) legally recognized 566 Native American tribes on May 2013 (U.S. Department of the Interior Indian Affairs, 2014). Given the large number of Native American nations, it is understandable that there is a wide range of funeral and mourning traditions. However, all have a strong emphasis on the importance of the natural world.

The Antiquities Act of 1906 infuriated many Native Americans. It allowed archeologists to disinter Native American gravesites. Museums and educational institutions removed skeletons and grave artifacts from original sites for study. However, in 1990, President George Bush signed the Native American Graves Protection and Repatriation Act establishing procedures and laws to return remains, funerary and sacred objects stored by agencies and museums, to the descendants' tribes. Following are some of the funeral and mourning practices of these 556 tribal groups.

The California tribes considered death as defilement that demanded purification ceremonies (Zimmerman, 2011, August 1). Many tribes practice cremation. Mourning consisted of singing and chanting that began as soon as the loved one died and continued for a day or often longer. Women and men cut their hair. The widow cut off all of her hair and burned it. Relatives burned the personal possessions and less elaborate homes of the deceased and avoided speaking the name of the deceased to prevent triggering grief. Tribe members joined together in ritual of communal mourning.

Hopi tribes venerate their ancestors and treat their physical remains with respect. Ancestors maintain a spiritual guardianship over burial sites (Ojibwa, 2013, March 18). The Hopi bury their dead as soon as possible because of their belief that any delay in burial of the deceased interferes with the soul's journey into the afterlife. A paternal aunt uses yucca shampoo to wash the deceased's hair and decorates the hair with prayer feathers. A mask representing clouds covers the face of the deceased. A woman is wrapped in her wedding robe; a man in a deerskin robe. The oldest son buries the deceased in seated position with offerings of food, water, and prayer sticks. He places a stick in the soil over the body to allow the soul to depart (Chavez III, 1999-2014, p. 5).

The Inuit tribal group in the Arctic region struggles to survive in one of the most forbidding territories on earth. According to an oral history gathered by Bennett and Rowley (2004), tribe members honor their dead in a five-day mourning ritual called "naasiivik," or the period of mourning. Death rituals include alerting others to a death in the home, carrying weapons to defend themselves in case of an encounter with evil spirits, and disposing of all of the deceased's belongings. Arctic tribe members hold fast to the idea that there is no real death, only a change in worlds.

Native Americans settled the Cahokia Mounds, a World Heritage Site around 600 CE. This settlement, across the Mississippi River from what is now St. Louis, Missouri faced serious health problems, including food supply and waste disposal. Archeologists studying the remains found in the mounds have identified one man, apparently an important ruler, interred in Mound 72, who they labeled the "falcon warrior" or "birdman" (*Cahokia*, 2014, August 15) The deceased, rested on a bed of more than 20,000 marine-shell disc beads arranged in the shape of a falcon. The burial mound also included a cache of arrowheads from four different geographical regions, demonstrating extensive trade links in North America. A steady supply of new immigrants brought there by social and political attractions balanced its high death rate. Apparently the city declined due to over-hunting and deforestation.

Members of the Navajo tribes believed the dead released their spirits when they died. They buried the bodies quickly upon death and often burned the homes and possessions of those who died. They perceived the death of a close relative as a dangerous time due to the great fear of souls who might return to the burial place or a former dwelling if not buried properly. Navajo believed the departed ghosts might be malevolent toward their own relatives (Nagel, 1988, p. 35). Members of some tribes avoided contact with the dying (Wilkie, 2003).

Navaho limit mourning to four days. During this period, relatives and friends of the deceased could talk about the deceased and express feelings of grief and sorrow, but the tribe disdained an excessive show of emotion. At the end of the four-day period, mourners resumed their usual routines with no further expression of emotion concerning the loss of the loved one. Involved in this restriction is the fear of the power of the dead person (Nagel, 1988, p. 35). Clements, Vigil, Manno, and Wilks (2003) noted that on the fourth day postmortem, relatives cleansed themselves thoroughly, as if washing away the need for further mourning. Navaho inter the deceased member's personal property with the corpse or destroy it. After the fourth day, mourners do not speak the name of the deceased, fearing that doing so would summon back the soul. Traditionally, they do not mention the deceased for one year following death. After this year, they rarely mention the name of the departed (Ojibwa, 2013, March 18, p.1).

Plains Tribes practiced *Aerial sepulture proper* (tree and scaffold burial) prior to European exploration and settlement in the Great Plains of the United States. Men only cut their hair when mourning the death of a close relative; however, the American government, public schools, and prisons have all forced Indian men to cut their hair in spite of the teachings of their tribal religions (Ojibwa, 2010, July 26, p.1).

Pueblo Tribe members placed food with the body of the deceased: a little food for those who had lived a good life and were going straight to the afterworld, more food for those who were destined for a more difficult journey (Ojibwa, 2013, March 18, p.1).

Native American funeral and mourning rituals vary widely. These tribes knew that death was always near, whether from hunger, disease, wild animals, accidents, or enemies (Advameg, Inc., 2014). While burial and mourning rituals passed from one nation to another through trade and intermarriage, each tribe maintained their own rituals and beliefs and adapted them to the ecology in which they lived.

Various Cultures
Funeral and Mourning Practices

People reportedly experience grief in similar ways across cultural boundaries (Cowles, 1966), though cultural traditions, beliefs, and values determine how they express grief and try to cope with it. As diversity increases in the American population, educators and health care professionals need to become culturally competent in all phases of interactions with minorities, especially when communicating with those who are grieving (Bougere, 2014).

Researchers agree that there is no "correct" way to mourn the loss of a loved one. Strategies to help people cope with death and mourning create the tapestry of every culture. "Beliefs, rituals, and traditions specific to a person's culture can provide some predictability and normalcy during a time that is difficult and confusing" (American Society of Clinical Oncology, 2014, p. 1).

Cultures impact how people express grief and mourning, and no two cultures exhibit exactly the same funeral and mourning rituals. Social norms determine individual tribal reaction to death including how people express grief. Response to the event depends on this cultural context and may help "define healthy pathways to new lives after trauma" (Griefspeaks.com, 2003, March, p. 3).

According to Gypsy or Romani tradition no one touches the dead person. Beeswax or pearls in the nose prevents evil spirits from entering the body. The gypsies destroy or sell everything the dead person owned to avoid contamination. Romani burn clothing, shatter belongings, and kill the deceased's animals other than horses (Patrin Web Journal, 2000). Like the Navajo, the Romani avoid saying the dead person's name (Wilkie, 2003) and are fearful that the dead may return to haunt the living.

Asian funerals may follow Buddhist, Confucian, or Taoist practices combined with some elements of Christian traditions (gathering at the funeral home to make arrangements, etc.). These rituals traditionally are long, intricate, beautiful, and respectful. Deference may include dressing the body in warm clothes, laying the deceased to rest in a watertight casket, and/or presenting the body in an open casket during the funeral. Poems written in calligraphy, chicken cooked as a last meal, traditional music, and burning incense at the grave are all funeral rituals designed to honor the deceased. Family members often create a shrine in the home to honor the loved one and display items related to the deceased (Griefspeaks.com, 2003, March).

Buddhists believe there is no need to fear death since death is merely a part of the circle of life (Hilgendorf, 2009, p.1). Buddhists mourn through meditation and prayers. Within a week after death Sri Lankan, Cambodian, and Thai Buddhists may hold up to three prayer meetings. Mourners view the body in its open casket and bow in respect (*How people of different cultures grieve*, 2010-2014, p. 1). Burning paper offerings (play money or pictures of mansions, Ferrari, or even computers) is one popular Buddhist ritual supports the tradition that the deceased will be able to use these in the afterlife. Buddhist cemeteries are home to two annual Chinese remembrance festivals of the dead: the Ching Ming Festival (Spring Remembrance) and the Chung Yeung Festival (Autumn Remembrance).

African-Americans draw from many cultures, ethnic groups, and religious traditions. The music and dancing of the jazz funeral in New Orleans help the deceased find a way to heaven and celebrate the final release of the deceased from the traumas of life on earth. Prior to the end of the Civil War, such joys included the release from slavery. Traditional instruments (tambourines and drums), coupled with the call-and-response style of singing and chanting, date back to funeral ceremonies that traveled across the Atlantic Ocean with African slaves. The music and dancing offer a cathartic release for mourners and a celebration of a life (Funeralwise LLC, 2014).

In Haiti, family members make the arrangements for the funeral and church services. Often there is a wake where family members and close friends meet at the home of the deceased to pray and offer support to each other. During the wake, people reminisce about the deceased, sharing favorite memories and music. On the day of the funeral, a viewing precedes the funeral service and graveside ceremonies. Close family members usually wear black or dark colors such as navy blue, purple, and brown since wearing bright colors like red, green, and yellow is inappropriate. Mourners often express their grief with great emotion. Family and friends usually hold a reception at the home of the deceased after the graveyard ceremony (Griefspeaks.com, 2003, March).

Because there is essentially no single "Hispanic culture," practices related to grief and bereavement differ (Bougere, 2014). Some Hispanics commemorate the loss of their loved ones with promises or commitments. These are very serious promises and failure to honor them is sinful. Friends and relatives often offer gifts of money to help cover the funeral expenses (Griefspeaks.com, 2003, March). Having a shrine, where family can come together to remember and celebrate the life of the loved one, is a key aspect in many Hispanic cultures. The detail and embellishment of the graves varies. Though cremation is increasing, most families still want a shrine where they can come to visit the deceased. Mexican funeral homes are now creating grand facilities to house cremation urns and family memorabilia (Griefspeaks.com, 2003, March).

There is a unique Jewish way of life and a Jewish way of death that manifests culturally specific attitudes about death and mourning. Jews turn to family and prayer while they mourn and show outward signs to promote healing within. They cover their mirrors, refrain from wearing shoes in the home, and men do not shave. Someone always watches over the body from the time of death until burial (Lamm, p. 4)

Jewish culture prohibits autopsies and embalming due to a profound respect for the body. Tradition proscribes open caskets, since Jews consider viewing the corpse disrespectful and unhelpful in the mitigation of grief. No funerals may occur on Saturday (the Sabbath) or on religious holidays. Funerals include eulogies, but music and flower arrangements are distractions. A contribution to charity or medical research is an appropriate remembrance.

Family members accompany the casket to the grave and are encouraged to place a shovel of earth on the casket as a sign of the finality of death. A set pattern of prayers after the death of a loved one speaks to the stages of grief. Post burial rituals include "three days of deep grief, seven days of mourning, thirty days of gradual readjustment, and eleven months of remembrance and healing" (as cited by Coleman, pp.136-137). Jews say the Kaddish, a declaration of faith, at the gravesite and during the seven-day mourning period following the burial; this is termed "sitting shiva." During this time, some Jewish families do not cook any food and keep a light burning to remember the loved one they have lost.

Many Jews wear a black pin with a torn ribbon or a torn garment during the funeral and for the next week, a symbol of their grief. They mark the first anniversary of the death by unveiling a tombstone at a special ceremony and the family gathers at the synagogue to light a candle that burns for 24 hours (*How People of Different Cultures Grieve*, n. d., p. 4). Rabbis discourage undue visiting the grave, but in a lovely tradition, the living pray that the dead will advocate for them as a "friend of the court" before the throne of God (Lamm, p. 195).

Christians trust they will go to heaven to be with God once they have died, and so, in some respects, a funeral is a time of both joy and sadness, as the person who will be missed by friends and loved ones is believed to have gone to a heavenly home. There are distinct phases to the Roman Catholic "Mass of Christian Burial": prayers are recited at the funeral home, the body is welcomed into the church, the casket is covered with a white cloth and sprinkled with holy water, the Eucharist is celebrated, prayers are recited, and the casket is escorted to the cemetery where the priest blesses the grave and says a few words of comfort to the mourners. Families may mark the death by requesting a memorial Mass (Griefspeaks.com, 2003, March).

Protestants often gather at the family home or funeral home. Caskets, open or closed, are an important part of the funeral ceremony. Cremation is an accepted option for some. For many, black dress is a part of mourning. Funeral services may include music and testimonials. Funeral attendees sing favorite inspirational hymns of praise. Gravesite rituals may be included in the funeral. Memorial services are becoming more common, sometimes replacing funerals. Flowers and donations remain preferred ways to express condolences. Church members and friends will usually assist in providing for the needs of the family, traditionally bringing food to the home of the immediate family. Many family members visit their loved one's graves to place flowers as a memorial (Griefspeaks.com, 2003, March).

Followers of Islam bury their loved ones in a Muslim cemetery. Only followers of Islam can lead the prayers. Prior to the funeral, the bathing of the body of the deceased following special traditions must occur, either at the mosque or the morgue. Ceremonies and prayers are included in the funeral. No coffin is required, since the body, wrapped simply in white clothes, must touch the earth. The face of deceased should look to the right toward Mecca. Islamic custom forbids women to visit the graveyard (Griefspeaks.com, 2003, March).

Faith, family, and community help Filipinos endure the poverty, diaspora, and tropical storms that routinely ravage their country. The Philippines is the only Christian nation in Asia – 86% identify as Roman Catholics. Mourning for the death of a loved one starts with a wake held in a funeral parlor or, more likely, the living room of a home. This is a place for quiet peaceful reflection. The family keeps a constant vigil while friends and neighbors pay their respects. Elsewhere in the house, people talk and share stories about the deceased. The family often sets aside a place for children to play games.

The wake lasts from three to seven days, especially if the family must await relatives from overseas. Mourners prepare and consume an abundance of food. Family members assume the expenses for food, drink, alcoholic beverages, lodging, and transportation for relatives. Some even purchase new white shirts for the male family members. Mourners sing, pray, play guitars, and gamble to keep family members awake. A generous portion of the winnings helps defray the cost of the wake. The community assists disadvantaged families. People may donate wood and nails for the coffin while local carpenters fashion it (Vistal).

Filipinos hold superstitions associated with funerals. The family dresses the body in simple clothes, no jewelry, or shoes. If they place a rosary in the coffin, they cut it to break the circle of death. Mourners wear black, although in accordance with modern

Catholic doctrine, they also wear white. No one wears red, a color reserved for joy. Filipinos consider it bad luck to disturb the coffin, allow the candles near the casket to expire, or carry food away from the wake.

A procession to the church takes place after the wake. The family rents jeepneys, a type of bus converted from a jeep, for the immediate family. Most people walk. A Roman Catholic priest offers the Mass of Christian Burial. The homily is less about the deceased and more about scripture. Funeral music is age appropriate. If the deceased is an important person in the community, the family provides a printed program.

Another procession takes place from the Church to the cemetery. Tradition dictates mourners take a different route than the one they took to the church. The priest blesses the gravesite and says a final prayer. Catholics offer a novena, a prayer for the deceased recited for nine-days beginning on the day of the death. A designated community member leads the novena. Mourners also say prayers at a forty-day remembrance and attend a one-year memorial Mass for the soul of the dead.

This review of funeral and mourning

practices shows that there is no correct way to mourn a loved one. Although some may seem strange when viewed through the lens of ethnocentrism, they all reflect deep-seated cultural norms and values. They support people in time of sorrow. They provide rituals and traditions that offer people predictability and normalcy following a tragic event.

Resources

Advameg, Inc. (2014). *Native American religion.* <http://www.deathreference>
American Society of Clinical Oncology. (2014). *Understanding grief within a cultural context.*<http://www.cancer.net/coping -and-emotions>
Aristotle, *Poetics.* (c. 335 BCE). Chapter 7, p. 1450b27.
 <http://www.identitytheory.com>
Axelrod, J. (2006). "The 5 stages of loss and grief." *PsychCenter,*
 <http://psychcentral.comlib/the-5-stages-of-loss-and-grief/000617.>
Bennett, J. & Rowley, S. (Eds.). (2004). *Uqalurait: An oral history of Nunavut.* Montreal: McGill-Queen's University Press.
Bougere, M. H. (2014). *Culture, grief, and bereavement: Applications for clinical practice.*
<http://www.minoritynurse.com>
Byock, I. (1997). *Dying well.* New York: Riverhead Publishers.
Cahokia. (2014, 15 August). http://en.wikipedia.org

Chavez III, F. B. (1999-2014). Hopi customs.< http://www.ehow.com/info_8575893->

Clements, P., Vigil, G., Manno, M., & Wilks, J. (2003). Cultural perspectives of death, grief, and bereavement. *Journal of Psychosocial Nursing and Mental Health Services*, 41(7), 18–26.

Coleman, P. (2011). *Corpses, coffins, and crypts*. New York: Holt and Company.

Cowles, K. V. (1996). Cultural perspectives of grief: An expanded concept analysis. *Journal of Advanced Nursing*, 23(2), 287-294.

Davis, C. (2014, May 27). "Thousands Pack Ala Moana Beach Park". *Star Advertiser*.

Durkheim, E. (1912). *The elementary forms of the religious life*. San Bernadino CA.

Elisabeth Kubler-Ross." (2014, February 17). < http://en.wikipedia.org>

Elisabeth Kubler Ross Foundation (2014). <http://www.ekrfoundation.org/>

Ferrer, D. (2014, August 5). Presentation at National Social Science Conference.

Funeralwise LLC. (2014). *New Orleans jazz funeral service rituals.*

<http://www.funeralwise.com/custom s/neworleans/>

Giesen, B. (2006). "Performing the sacred." p. 325, in Giesen, B., Alexander J., and Mast, J. Eds. *Social performance: symbolic action, cultural perspectives and ritual.* Cambridge University Press: Cambridge (UK).

Griefspeaks.com. (2003, March). *Understanding cultural issues in death.* <http://griefspeaks.com/id90.html>

Henslin, J. (2003). *Sociology: A down-to-earth approach.* Boston: Pearson Publishing.

Hilgendorf, A. (2009, June 24). *Does culture dictate the grieving process?* p.1. <http://ezinearticles.com>

How people of different cultures grieve. (2010-2014). p.1. <http://www.smartinfo.me>

Huang, J. (2000). *Death: Cultural traditions.* <http://www.pbs.org/wnet>

Interview at Shinnyo-en Buddhist temple. (2014, 22 May at 4:00 pm) 1953 South Beretania Street, Honolulu, Hawaii with the Reverend Reiko Hori, Charlene Ide Flanter, and Martin Hosch, Global Project Manager.

Kellehear, A. (2014). "On death and dying." <http://www.ekfroundation.org/.>

Kumar, S. M. (2005). *Grieving mindfully.* Oakland, CA: New Harbinger.

Lamm, M. (2000). *The Jewish way in death and mourning,* New York: Jonathon David Publishers.

Lantern Floating Hawaii (2014). [pamphlet] Memorial Day, Honolulu Hawaii.

Lewis, C. S. (1961). *A grief observed.* New York: Harper.

Lynch, G. (2012, December 24). Emile Durkheim: *The Manchester Guardian.*

May, K. T. (2013). *11 fascinating funeral traditions from around the globe.* <http://blog.ted.com/2013/10/01/11>

Nagel, J. K. (1988). Unresolved grief and mourning in Navajo women. *American Indian and Alaska Native Mental Health Research,* 2(2), 32-40.

Ojibwa. (2013, March 18). *Death in Pueblo and Athabascan cultures,* p. 1. <http://nativeamericannetroots.net/diary>

Ojibwa. (2010, July 26). *Long hair.* p.1. <http://nativeamericannetroots.net/diary/601>

Patricelli, K. (1995-2015). "Stage of grief models: Kubler-Ross." *AMHC.* <http://www.amhc.org>

Patrin Web Journal. (2000). *Romani customs and traditions: Death rituals and customs.*

<http://www.reocities.com/~patrin/death>.

Tribal Directory. (2015). <http://www.bia.gov/>

Tsai, M. (2013, May 28). "Messages of love, aloha" *Star Advertiser.*

Turner, V. (1975). *Dramas, fields, and metaphors.* London: Cornell Press.

Turner, V. (1982). *Ritual to theater.* New York: PAJ Publications.

Vimeo Video. (2014). Lantern Floating Hawaii <http://lanternfloatinghawaii.com>

Vistal, F. (2015, June 8). Interview at Interfaith Chapel, Veterans Outreach and Clinics.

Wilkie, D. J. (2003). *TNEEL self study: Grief: Sociocultural aspects.* <http://www.tneel.uic.edu/tneel-ss/demo/grief/frame1.asp>

Wolterstorff, N. (1987). *Lament for a son.* Grand Rapids: Eerdmans Publishing.

Zimmerman, F. (2011, August 1). *California Native Americans: Customs and religion.* <http://americanindianshistory.blogspot.com/2011/09>

Zoelick, S. (2012, May 29). "Flickers of comfort and hope." *Star Advertiser,* p. A6, c. 2.

About the Authors

Patricia M. Kirtley lives in Medford, Oregon. She earned a Master of Fine Arts Degree in Writing Children's Literature from Vermont College of Fine Arts. She also worked in a hospital laboratory for 40 years as a Medical Technologist, MT (ASCP). She serves on the Board of Directors of the National Social Science Association.

Lem Londos Railsback lives and writes in Laredo, Texas. A lifelong educator, Dr. Railsback holds a Ph.D. in Compensatory C & L: Linguistics & Reading all-levels. He has published a number of works including *Albu De La Cibola.* Recently retired after 50 years of teaching, he won the coveted Citizen of the Year Award for lifetime achievement from the National Social Science awarded in 2015.

William Madison Kirtley lives in Medford, Oregon. He earned a Doctor of Arts in Political Science from Idaho State University. His book, *The Politics of Death* deals with the origins of Oregon's Death With Dignity Act. He recently retired from teaching sailors college classes aboard deployed US Navy ships. He is currently President of the National Social Studies Association.

William (Bill) R. Curtis is a retired Army chief warrant officer IV who served over 31 years in the military; he is happily mowing his acreage and supporting his wife's landscaping projects. He is a member of the board of the National Social Science Association.

Terry L. Lovelace, Ph. D., is a retired elementary education professor now residing on the Gulf Coast in Mississippi, nurturing azaleas and camellias and her husband Bill. She is a past President of the National Social Science Association.